WILD WICKED WONDERFUL

TOP 10:

ODDITIES

By Virginia Loh-Hagan

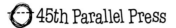
45th Parallel Press

Published in the United States of America by Cherry Lake Publishing
Ann Arbor, Michigan
www.cherrylakepublishing.com

Content Adviser: Stephen Ditchkoff, Professor of Wildlife Ecology and Management, Auburn University, Alabama
Reading Adviser: Marla Conn, ReadAbility, Inc.
Book Designer: Melinda Millward

Photo Credits: © Seatraveler/Dreamstime.com, cover, 1, 7; © Piyus Silaban/Dreamstime.com, 5, 18; ©Berendje Photography/Shutterstock Images, 6; ©Edwin Butter/Shutterstock Images, 6; ©Richard Whitcombe/Shutterstock Images, 6; ©Ryan M. Bolton/Shutterstock Images, 8; ©Parkpoom Photography/Shutterstock Images, 10; ©Suede Chen/Shutterstock Images, 11; ©ivkuzmin/iStockphoto, 12; ©worldswildlifewonders/Shutterstock Images, 12; ©nattanan726/Shutterstock Images, 12; ©Vilainecrevette/Shutterstock Images, 13; ©Ivan Kuzmin/Shutterstock Images, 14; ©breakermaximus/Shutterstock Images, 15; ©swedishmonica/Thinkstock, 16; ©feathercollector/Shutterstock Images, 16, 17; ©Andrea Izzotti/Shutterstock Images, 18; ©Worakit Sirijinda/Shutterstock Images, 18; ©Jennifer Brady/Dreamstime.com, 19; ©Jana Shea/Shutterstock Images, 20; ©Ethan Daniels/Shutterstock Images, 20; ©Virunja/Shutterstock Images, 20; ©Jarous/Shutterstock Images, 21; © Paul Starosta/Corbis, 22, 23; ©javarman/Shutterstock Images, 24; ©dennisvdwater/Canstock, 24; ©dennisvdw/Thinkstock, 25; ©Johncarnemolla/Dreamstime.com, 26; © David Watts/Visuals Unlimited/Corbis, 27; © Kasparart/Dreamstime.com, 28; ©NOAA/NMFS/SEFSC Pascagoula Laboratory; Collection of Brandi Noble, NOAA/NMFS/SEFSC/ http://www.flickr.com/ CC-BY-2.0, 28; © Norbert Wu/ Minden Pictures/Newscom, 29; © Bluegreen Pictures / Alamy Stock Photo, 30

Graphic Element Credits: © tukkki/Shutterstock Images, back cover, front cover, multiple interior pages; © paprika/Shutterstock Images, back cover, front cover, multiple interior pages; © Silhouette Lover/Shutterstock Images, multiple interior pages

45th Parallel Press is an imprint of Cherry Lake Publishing.

Library of Congress Cataloging-in-Publication Data

Loh-Hagan, Virginia, author.
   Top 10 : oddities / by Virginia Loh-Hagan.
pages cm. — (Wild wicked wonderful)
ISBN 978-1-63470-504-2 (hardcover) — ISBN 978-1-63470-624-7 (pbk.) —
ISBN 978-1-63470-564-6 (pdf) — ISBN 978-1-63470-684-1 (ebook)
1. Animals—Juvenile literature. I. Title. II. Title: Top ten : oddities. III. Title: Oddities.

QL49.L835 2016
590—dc23   2015026856

Printed in the United States of America
Corporate Graphics

About the Author

Dr. Virginia Loh-Hagan is an author, university professor, former classroom teacher, and curriculum designer. She loves all the odd things about her friends. Odd is special! Odd is cool! She lives in San Diego with her very tall husband and very naughty dogs. To learn more about her, visit www.virginialoh.com.

TABLE OF CONTENTS

INTRODUCTION

Animals are odd. They look odd. They do odd things. They stand out. They're special.

They're odd for different reasons. They develop ways to **survive**. Survive means to stay alive. They're built for their **environment**. Environment means their homes. They **adapt** to where they live. Adapt means change. Being odd is key. That's how they hunt. That's how they eat. That's how they protect themselves.

Some animals are extreme **oddities**. Oddities are strange things. Their looks are odder than most. Their **habits** are odder than most. Habits are ways of doing things. They're the most exciting oddities in the animal world!

Over time, animals have evolved, or changed, to survive.

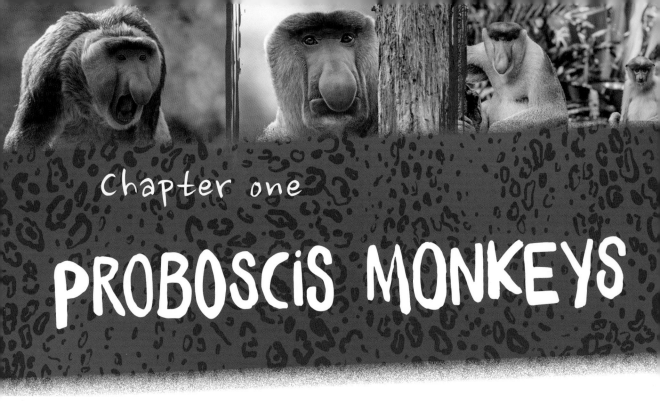

Chapter one

PROBOSCIS MONKEYS

Proboscis monkeys live in groups. A proboscis is a long, moving nose. Each group of monkeys has one male. It has several females. It includes their kids. Males look different from females. Males can be 50 pounds (22.7 kilograms). Females are half that size.

Males have odd noses. Males have big noses. Their noses hang low. They're lower than their mouths. They use their noses. They attract mates. Females have smaller noses. They like big noses.

Male proboscis monkeys' noses slowly grow until adulthood.

Males' noses help them honk. Larger noses make sounds louder. Males guard their space by honking. They scare other males. They also use honking to impress females.

Proboscis monkeys are the largest of Asia's monkeys.

These monkeys live in Borneo. Borneo is the largest island in Asia. They live in forests. They live mostly in trees. They go to the ground to search for food. They're shy. They're hairy. They're good swimmers. They have webbed feet and hands.

The monkeys have **potbellies**. They have big stomachs. Their stomachs stick out.

They mainly eat leaves, seeds, and unripe fruits. They have an odd eating system. They chew **cud**. Their stomachs are divided into parts. They let food get soft in their stomachs. They throw up large bits. They chew again. Chewing breaks down food.

Humans Do What?!?

Michel Lotito was known as "Mr. Eats All." He ate 18 bikes. He ate 15 shopping carts. He ate seven televisions. He ate two beds. He took two years to eat an airplane. He took these things apart. He cut them up. He drank mineral oil. He swallowed the things. He drank lots of water. This made things go down easier. He began eating these things at age 16. He ate 2.2 pounds (1 kg) of these things every day. In his lifetime, he ate 9 tons of metal. He has no bad effects from his strange diet. A diet is what people eat. He had pica. This is a medical condition. It causes people to crave dirt, glass, and metal. Pica can cause blockage, lead poisoning, and damage. But Lotito's stomach was odd. His stomach walls were double thick. His stomach juices were powerful. Sharp things could pass through his body.

chapter two

STALK-EYED FLiES

Male stalk-eyed flies have odd eyes. Their eyes stick out. They stick out half the length of the body. They're on **stalks**. Stalks are like rods. They stick out from each side of their head.

Their eyes are wide apart. Wider is better. Longer stalks are better. Bigger males have wider eyes. They attract more females. They scare off other males.

Sometimes, males fight. They fight for females. Males face each other. They compare eye **spans**. Spans are the distances between things. They spread their front legs

Stalk-eyed flies are about
0.4 inches (1 cm) long.

apart. This makes their eyes look wider.

Females don't have stalks. They want males with extreme
eyes.

chapter three
SLOTHS

Sloths live in jungles. They live in Central and South America. They have an odd way of hanging out. They spend their lives upside down. They hang by their claws. Their claws are long and curved. They have strong grips. They don't fall down. They stay hanging even after death.

They do everything upside down. They eat. They sleep. They mate. Their organs are upside down. Their fur grows upside down.

Sloths can't walk upright on the ground.

Sloths have slow digestive systems. They only need to use the bathroom once a week. They leave their trees to do this. They go on the ground.

Sloths move very slowly.

Sloths have odd fur. They have thick fur. This helps them float. They're good swimmers. Their home floods a lot. So, being able to swim is good.

Their fur has special grooves. **Algae** grow in their hair. Algae are like plants. Algae helps sloths hide. They blend into the trees. This keeps **predators** away. Predators are hunters.

Their fur is a home. It houses more than 100 moths. These sloth moths lay eggs in sloth **dung**. Dung is poop. Moths wait for sloths to use the bathroom. They quickly lay eggs. Then they get back on the sloths.

When Animals Attack!

People are scared of the "Vampire Beast of North Carolina." This animal is blamed for killing animals. It mainly killed dogs. It crushed their heads. It tore their bodies. It drained blood from their dead bodies. In 1953, the beast killed many dogs. It drained their blood. Farmers hunted the beast. But the killings stopped. In 2003, the beast came back. It killed many pit bulls and other animals. It drained their blood. Then it stopped killing. In 2013, the beast came back again. It killed horses. It killed big dogs. It killed other animals. It cut the animals' necks. It drained their blood. It seems to come and go. People say it has the body of a bear and the head of a cat. The beast is said to be 5 feet (152.4 cm) long. It's black. Experts say it doesn't exist. People are probably seeing a wildcat.

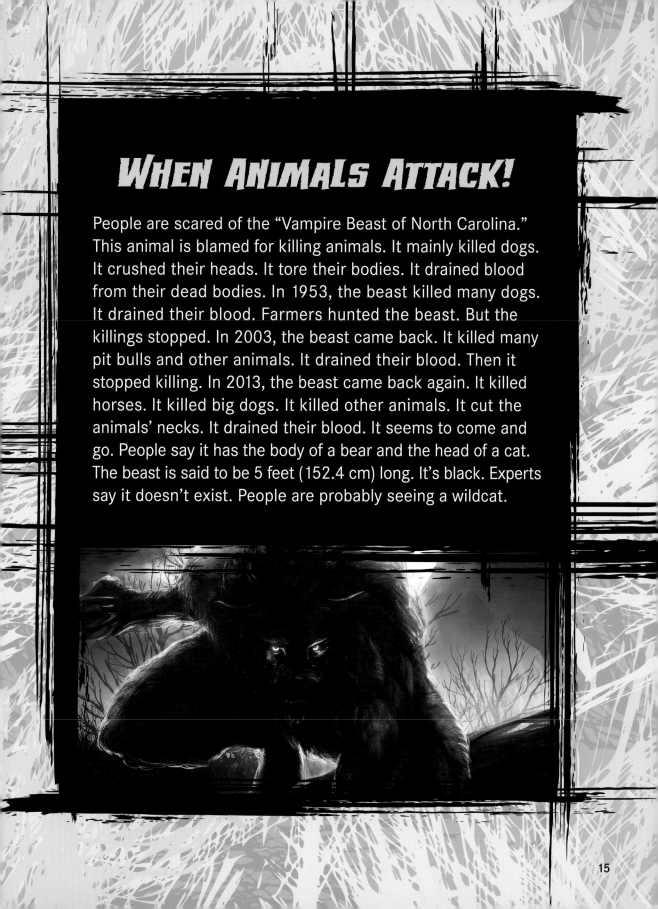

chapter four
FLYING FISH

Flying fish live in the Atlantic Ocean. They're **prey**. Prey are animals hunted for food. Flying fish developed an odd way to escape predators.

Flying fish have fins. These fins are on each side. They're behind the **gills**. Gills are breathing organs.

They have extra-large fins. Their fins are as long as their bodies. They're the size of a small bird's wings. They're used for jumping. They're used for gliding. It looks like they're flying over the water surface.

Flying fish can glide farther than the length of a football field.

They beat their tails. They do this up to 50 times a second.
They go more than 30 miles (48 kilometers) per hour.

Chapter five

CASSOWARIES

Cassowaries live in jungles. They live in northern Australia. They look odd.

Their **crests** help them run. Crests are the top part of a bird's head. A cassowary crest is like a helmet. Cassowaries stretch out their crests. They avoid vines. They avoid predators. They speed through the jungle. They go 30 miles (48 km) per hour. They jump 5 feet (152.4 cm). Crests protect their heads.

They have strong legs. They're 6 feet (183 cm) tall. They weigh as much as adult humans. They can't fly. They don't have a bone in their chest for flight muscles. They're too big to fly.

Cassowaries are fast runners.

Chapter six
HORSESHOE CRABS

Horseshoe crabs are more than 450 million years old. They're older than dinosaurs. They're also not crabs. They are related more to spiders.

They're very odd. They have 12 legs. They have 10 eyes. They can see light that humans can't see. And their blood is baby blue! It protects them. It traps germs. Germs can't spread.

Scientists don't know much about them. They can only study them in June. Crabs appear when the new moon

Horseshoe crabs are living fossils.

rises. Thousands of these crabs come out. They leave the sea. They go to the sand. Females drag the males. They mate. Then they disappear.

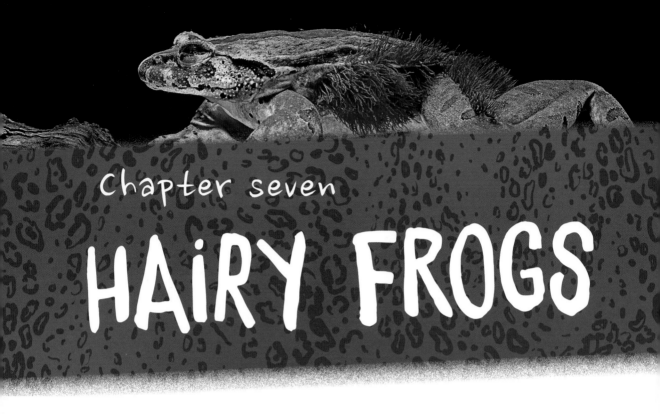

Chapter seven

HAIRY FROGS

Hairy frogs live in waterfalls. They live in West and Central Africa. Frogs with hair are odd. Males have hair on their body. They have hair on their thighs.

They have small lungs. Their hairs help them breathe. They're like gills. They hold blood. They take in oxygen from the water. Their hair only appears during mating.

Females lay eggs underwater. Males look after the eggs. They stay with the eggs. Their hairy bottoms help them breathe. The males can spend more time underwater. They stay until the eggs hatch. Then their hair falls off.

Hairy frogs are also called horror frogs or wolverine frogs.

Hairy frogs also have claws. They're made of bone. They push the claws out. The claws come out of their skin. They have to break their toes to do it.

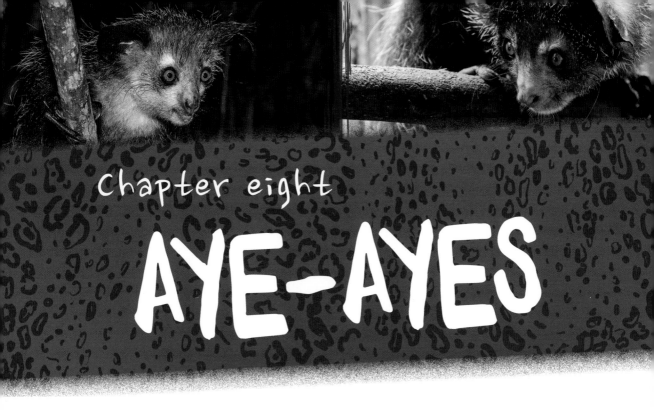

Chapter eight

AYE-AYES

Aye-ayes are **primates**. Primates include humans, apes, and monkeys. Aye-ayes look odd. Their heads look like **rodents**. Rodents include rats and mice. Aye-ayes have beaver teeth. They have bat ears. They have fox tails. They have monkey bodies.

They're lemurs. They're **nocturnal**. They hunt at night. They live in Madagascar.

They eat like woodpeckers. They have skinny hands. They have bony middle fingers. Their middle fingers are long. They're three times longer than their other fingers. They

Aye-ayes spend most of their lives in trees.

tap on wood. They listen for sounds. They bite holes in the wood. They use their middle fingers to dig out bugs.

Chapter nine
PLATYPUSES

Platypuses live in rivers. They live in Australia. They have duck **bills**. Bills are beaks. They have mole bodies. They have beaver tails. They have otter feet. They may look odd. But they're built to hunt underwater.

They swim. They use their webbed feet. They steer with their tails. They close their eyes, ears, and nose. They have special feelers on their bills. They can feel prey's movements.

Mammals have fur. Birds lay eggs. Platypuses are so odd. They combine both animal types. They're egg-laying mammals.

Folds of skin cover platypuses' eyes and ears to prevent water from entering. Their nostrils are sealed closed.

Males are poisonous. They have sharp stingers. The stingers are on their heels. They're on their back feet.

Chapter ten
ANGLERFISH

Anglerfish are bony fish. They live thousands of feet below the sea. They live in icy black water.

Females go fishing for fish. They have something coming out of their foreheads. It looks like a fishing rod. It has millions of bacteria. It makes light. Anglerfish use it like a **lure**. They draw other fish in. Then they eat them. They also use these rods to attract males.

Females are predators. They have big heads. They have long teeth. Their teeth look like fangs. They have flexible stomachs. They can swallow prey twice their size.

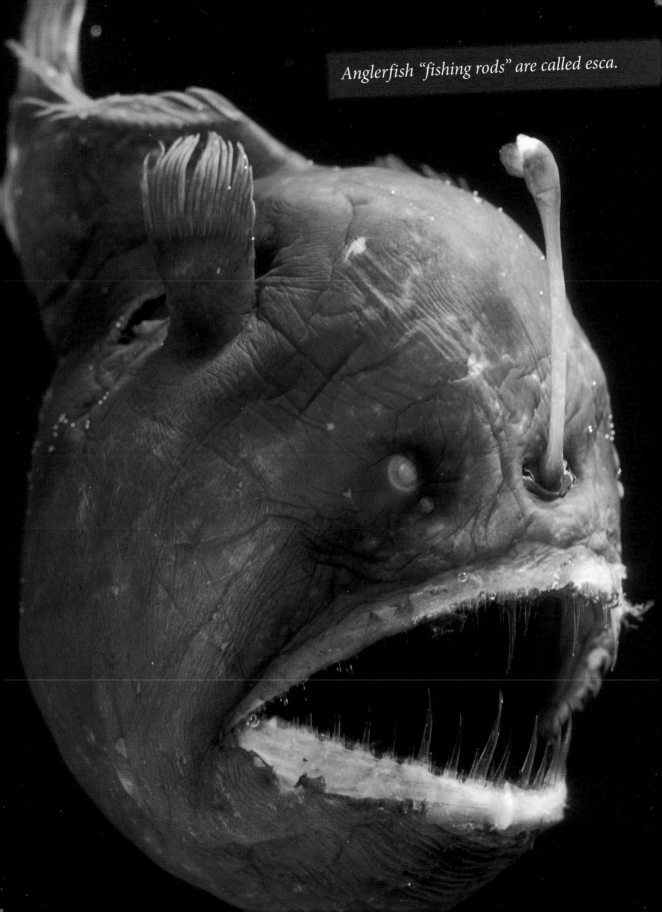

Anglerfish "fishing rods" are called esca.

Scientists thought females had strange bumps. They didn't realize those bumps were male anglerfish.

Males are 40 times smaller than females. They have tiny teeth. They don't have any guts. They don't have rods. They're weak. They have an odd way of surviving.

They grab females. They bite into their skins. Then their body breaks down. Their jaws join into the females' skin. Their blood veins do the same. Males become bumps. They live on females' bodies. They depend on females for food. They depend on females for their lives.

This is also how anglerfish mate. Males become bigger when they're attached to females. They give females babies.